**Great Works** **Instructional Guides** for **Literature**

The Adventures of Tom Sawyer

A guide for the novel by Mark Twain
Great Works Author: Suzanne Barchers

SHELL EDUCATION

Publishing Credits

Corinne Burton, M.A.Ed., *President*; Emily R. Smith, M.A.Ed., *Editorial Director*; Lee Aucoin, *Multimedia Designer*; Stephanie Bernard, *Assistant Editor*; Don Tran, *Production Artist*; Amber Goff, *Editorial Assistant*

Image Credits

© GraphicaArtis/Worth Brehm/Corbis (cover)

Standards

© 2007 Teachers of English to Speakers of Other Languages, Inc. (TESOL)
© 2007 Board of Regents of the University of Wisconsin System. World-Class Instructional Design and Assessment (WIDA)
© Copyright 2010. National Governors Association Center for Best Practices and Council of Chief State School Officers. All rights reserved.

Shell Education

5301 Oceanus Drive
Huntington Beach, CA 92649-1030
http://www.shelleducation.com

ISBN 978-1-4258-8973-9

© 2015 Shell Educational Publishing, Inc.

Printed in USA. WOR004

Table of Contents

How to Use This Literature Guide

Today's standards demand rigor and relevance in the reading of complex texts. The units in this series guide teachers in a rich and deep exploration of worthwhile works of literature for classroom study. The most rigorous instruction can also be interesting and engaging!

Many current strategies for effective literacy instruction have been incorporated into these instructional guides for literature. Throughout the units, text-dependent questions are used to determine comprehension of the book as well as student interpretation of the vocabulary words. The books chosen for the series are complex exemplars of carefully crafted works of literature. Close reading is used throughout the units to guide students toward revisiting the text and using textual evidence to respond to prompts orally and in writing. Students must analyze the story elements in multiple assignments for each section of the book. All of these strategies work together to rigorously guide students through their study of literature.

The next few pages will make clear how to use this guide for a purposeful and meaningful literature study. Each section of this guide is set up in the same way to make it easier for you to implement the instruction in your classroom.

Theme Thoughts

The great works of literature used throughout this series have important themes that have been relevant to people for many years. Many of the themes will be discussed during the various sections of this instructional guide. However, it would also benefit students to have independent time to think about the key themes of the novel.

Before students begin reading, have them complete *Pre-Reading Theme Thoughts* (page 13). This graphic organizer will allow students to think about the themes outside the context of the story. They'll have the opportunity to evaluate statements based on important themes and defend their opinions. Be sure to have students keep their papers for comparison to the *Post-Reading Theme Thoughts* (page 64). This graphic organizer is similar to the pre-reading activity. However, this time, students will be answering the questions from the point of view of one of the characters in the novel. They have to think about how the character would feel about each statement and defend their thoughts. To conclude the activity, have students compare what they thought about the themes before they read the novel to what the characters discovered during the story.

How to Use This Literature Guide (cont.)

Vocabulary

Each teacher overview page has definitions and sentences about how key vocabulary words are used in the section. These words should be introduced and discussed with students. There are two student vocabulary activity pages in each section. On the first page, students are asked to define the ten words chosen by the author of this unit. On the second page in most sections, each student will select at least eight words that he or she finds interesting or difficult. For each section, choose one of these pages for your students to complete. With either assignment, you may want to have students get into pairs to discuss the meanings of the words. Allow students to use reference guides to define the words. Monitor students to make sure the definitions they have found are accurate and relate to how the words are used in the text.

On some of the vocabulary student pages, students are asked to answer text-related questions about the vocabulary words. The following question stems will help you create your own vocabulary questions if you'd like to extend the discussion.

- How does this word describe _____'s character?

- In what ways does this word relate to the problem in this story?

- How does this word help you understand the setting?

- In what ways is this word related to the story's solution?

- Describe how this word supports the novel's theme of . . . .

- What visual images does this word bring to your mind?

- For what reasons might the author have chosen to use this particular word?

At times, more work with the words will help students understand their meanings. The following quick vocabulary activities are a good way to further study the words.

- Have students practice their vocabulary and writing skills by creating sentences and/or paragraphs in which multiple vocabulary words are used correctly and with evidence of understanding.

- Students can play vocabulary concentration. Students make a set of cards with the words and a separate set of cards with the definitions. Then, students lay the cards out on the table and play concentration. The goal of the game is to match vocabulary words with their definitions.

- Students can create word journal entries about the words. Students choose words they think are important and then describe why they think each word is important within the novel.

How to Use This Literature Guide (cont.)

Analyzing the Literature

After students have read each section, hold small-group or whole-class discussions. Questions are written at two levels of complexity to allow you to decide which questions best meet the needs of your students. The Level 1 questions are typically less abstract than the Level 2 questions. Level 1 is indicated by a square, while Level 2 is indicated by a triangle. These questions focus on the various story elements, such as character, setting, and plot. Student pages are provided if you want to assign these questions for individual student work before your group discussion. Be sure to add further questions as your students discuss what they've read. For each question, a few key points are provided for your reference as you discuss the novel with students.

Reader Response

In today's classrooms, there are often great readers who are below-average writers. So much time and energy is spent in classrooms getting students to read on grade level that little time is left to focus on writing skills. To help teachers include more writing in their daily literacy instruction, each section of this guide has a literature-based reader response prompt. Each of the three genres of writing is used in the reader responses within this guide: narrative, informative/explanatory, and opinion/argument. Students have a choice between two prompts for each reader response. One response requires students to make connections between the reading and their own lives. The other prompt requires students to determine text-to-text connections or connections within the text.

Close Reading the Literature

Within each section, students are asked to closely reread a short section of text. Since some versions of the novels have different page numbers, the selections are described by chapter and location, along with quotations to guide the readers. After each close reading, there are text-dependent questions to be answered by students.

Encourage students to read each question one at a time and then go back to the text and discover the answer. Work with students to ensure that they use the text to determine their answers rather than making unsupported inferences. Once students have answered the questions, discuss what they discovered. Suggested answers are provided in the answer key.

How to Use This Literature Guide (cont.)

Close Reading the Literature (cont.)

The generic, open-ended stems below can be used to write your own text-dependent questions if you would like to give students more practice.

- Give evidence from the text to support . . . .
- Justify your thinking using text evidence about . . . .
- Find evidence to support your conclusions about . . . .
- What text evidence helps the reader understand . . . ?
- Use the book to tell why _____ happens.
- Based on events in the story, ...
- Use text evidence to describe why . . . .

Making Connections

The activities in this section help students make cross-curricular connections to writing, mathematics, science, social studies, or the fine arts. Each of these types of activities requires higher-order thinking skills from students.

Creating with the Story Elements

It is important to spend time discussing the common story elements in literature. Understanding the characters, setting, and plot can increase students' comprehension and appreciation of the story. If teachers discuss these elements daily, students will more likely internalize the concepts and look for the elements in their independent reading. Another important reason for focusing on the story elements is that students will be better writers if they think about how the stories they read are constructed.

Students are given three options for working with the story elements. They are asked to create something related to the characters, setting, or plot of the novel. Students are given a choice in this activity so that they can decide to complete the activity that most appeals to them. Different multiple intelligences are used so that the activities are diverse and interesting to all students.

How to Use This Literature Guide (cont.)

Culminating Activity

This open-ended, cross-curricular activity requires higher-order thinking and allows for a creative product. Students will enjoy getting the chance to share what they have discovered through reading the novel. Be sure to allow them enough time to complete the activity at school or home.

Comprehension Assessment

The questions in this section are modeled after current standardized tests to help students analyze what they've read and prepare for tests they may see in their classrooms. The questions are dependent on the text and require critical-thinking skills to answer.

Response to Literature

The final post-reading activity is an essay based on the text that also requires further research by students. This is a great way to extend this book into other curricular areas. A suggested rubric is provided for teacher reference.

Correlation to the Standards

Shell Education is committed to producing educational materials that are research and standards based. As part of this effort, we have correlated all of our products to the academic standards of all 50 states, the District of Columbia, the Department of Defense Dependents Schools, and all Canadian provinces.

Purpose and Intent of Standards

Standards are designed to focus instruction and guide adoption of curricula. Standards are statements that describe the criteria necessary for students to meet specific academic goals. They define the knowledge, skills, and content students should acquire at each level. Standards are also used to develop standardized tests to evaluate students' academic progress. Teachers are required to demonstrate how their lessons meet standards. Standards are used in the development of all of our products, so educators can be assured they meet high academic standards.

How to Find Standards Correlations

To print a customized correlation report of this product for your state, visit our website at http://www.shelleducation.com and follow the online directions. If you require assistance in printing correlation reports, please contact our Customer Service Department at 1-877-777-3450.

Correlation to the Standards (cont.)

Standards Correlation Chart

The lessons in this book were written to support today's college and career readiness standards. The following chart indicates which lessons address each standard.

College and Career Readiness Standard	Section
Read closely to determine what the text says explicitly and to make logical inferences from it; cite specific textual evidence when writing or speaking to support conclusions drawn from the text. (R.1)	Close Reading the Literature Sections 1–5; Culminating Activity
Determine central ideas or themes of a text and analyze their development; summarize the key supporting details and ideas. (R.2)	Analyzing the Literature Sections 1–5; Creating with the Story Elements Sections 1–5; Making Connections Sections 2–4; Culminating Activity; Post-Reading Response to Literature
Analyze how and why individuals, events, or ideas develop and interact over the course of a text. (R.3)	Analyzing the Literature Sections 1–5; Creating with the Story Elements Sections 1–5; Making Connections Section 3; Culminating Activity; Post-Reading Response to Literature
Interpret words and phrases as they are used in a text, including determining technical, connotative, and figurative meanings, and analyze how specific word choices shape meaning or tone. (R.4)	Vocabulary Sections 1–5; Close Reading the Literature Sections 1–5
Analyze the structure of texts, including how specific sentences, paragraphs, and larger portions of the text (e.g., a section, chapter, scene, or stanza) relate to each other and the whole. (R.5)	Analyzing the Literature Sections 1–5; Creating with the Story Elements Sections 1–5
Assess how point of view or purpose shapes the content and style of a text. (R.6)	Post-Reading Theme Thoughts; Culminating Activity; Post-Reading Response to Literature
Read and comprehend complex literary and informational texts independently and proficiently. (R.10)	Entire Unit
Write arguments to support claims in an analysis of substantive topics or texts using valid reasoning and relevant and sufficient evidence. (W.1)	Reader Response Sections 1–5; Culminating Activity; Post-Reading Response to Literature
Write informative/explanatory texts to examine and convey complex ideas and information clearly and accurately through the effective selection, organization, and analysis of content. (W.2)	Reader Response Sections 1–2; Culminating Activity; Post-Reading Response to Literature
Write narratives to develop real or imagined experiences or events using effective technique, well-chosen details and well-structured event sequences. (W.3)	Reader Response Sections 3–5
Produce clear and coherent writing in which the development, organization, and style are appropriate to task, purpose, and audience. (W.4)	Reader Response Sections 1–5; Culminating Activity; Post-Reading Response to Literature
Use technology, including the Internet, to produce and publish writing and to interact and collaborate with others. (W.6)	Creating with the Story Elements Section 1; Making Connections Section 2
Conduct short as well as more sustained research projects based on focused questions, demonstrating understanding of the subject under investigation. (W.7)	Making Connections Section 2
Draw evidence from literary or informational texts to support analysis, reflection, and research. (W.9)	Culminating Activity; Making Connections Section 2; Post-Reading Response to Literature

Correlation to the Standards (cont.)

Standards Correlation Chart (cont.)

College and Career Readiness Standard	Section
Write routinely over extended time frames (time for research, reflection, and revision) and shorter time frames (a single sitting or a day or two) for a range of tasks, purposes, and audiences. (W.10)	Reader Response Sections 1–5; Culminating Activity; Post-Reading Response to Literature
Demonstrate command of the conventions of standard English grammar and usage when writing or speaking. (L.1)	Reader Response Sections 1–5; Culminating Activity; Post-Reading Response to Literature
Demonstrate command of the conventions of standard English capitalization, punctuation, and spelling when writing. (L.2)	Reader Response Sections 1–5; Culminating Activity; Post-Reading Response to Literature
Apply knowledge of language to understand how language functions in different contexts, to make effective choices for meaning or style, and to comprehend more fully when reading or listening. (L.3)	Vocabulary Sections 1–5; Reader Response Section 1–5
Determine or clarify the meaning of unknown and multiple-meaning words and phrases by using context clues, analyzing meaningful word parts, and consulting general and specialized reference materials, as appropriate. (L.4)	Vocabulary Sections 1–5
Demonstrate understanding of figurative language, word relationships, and nuances in word meanings. (L.5)	Vocabulary Sections 1–5
Acquire and use accurately a range of general academic and domain-specific words and phrases sufficient for reading, writing, speaking, and listening at the college and career readiness level; demonstrate independence in gathering vocabulary knowledge when encountering an unknown term important to comprehension or expression. (L.6)	Vocabulary Sections 1–5; Reader Response Section 1–5

TESOL and WIDA Standards

The lessons in this book promote English language development for English language learners. The following TESOL and WIDA English Language Development Standards are addressed through the activities in this book:

- Standard 1: English language learners communicate for social and instructional purposes within the school setting.
- Standard 2: English language learners communicate information, ideas and concepts necessary for academic success in the content area of language arts.

About the Author—Samuel Longhorn Clemens a.k.a. Mark Twain

Born on November 30, 1835, in Florida, Missouri, Samuel Clemens was the sixth of seven children. The family moved to Hannibal, Missouri, when Clemens was four years old. The proximity to the Mississippi River proved to be a primary influence on Clemens's development and life choices.

After his father's death in 1847, Clemens went to work as a printer's apprentice. He'd only completed the fifth grade, but this job proved to be a great source of continuing education. Working for a local newspaper, he had ready access to the world through news stories. This was the first of many jobs for Clemens. After working as a writer for newspapers in New York City and Philadelphia, he returned to Missouri to become an apprentice on a steamboat. With the outbreak of the Civil War, river traffic halted, and Clemens volunteered for a short time in a Confederate unit. After his brief voluntary work, Clemens headed west to make a living as a miner and prospector.

Failing to strike it rich out West, Clemens turned to writing again. He began using the pen name of Mark Twain. Clemens got the name from his time spent on riverboats. A rope was used to mark the depth of the water, ensuring that the boat would not run aground. Calling out "mark twain" while measuring indicated that the water was two fathoms (12 feet; 3.7 meters) deep, thus safe for passage.

Clemens found an audience for his articles and short stories, which led to him traveling far and wide. While on his first trip to Europe, he met Charles Langdon, who showed him a picture of his sister, Olivia. Clemens courted Olivia for years. They married and moved to Hartford, Connecticut, where they raised their family. Olivia served as Clemens's unofficial editor. For the next 17 years, Clemens lived in Hartford writing beloved books such as *The Adventures of Tom Sawyer*, *The Prince and the Pauper*, *A Connecticut Yankee in King Arthur's Court*, and *The Adventures of Huckleberry Finn*.

Clemens drew upon his rich store of experiences for his writings, even as he faced financial difficulty, became disillusioned with the American government, and dealt with losing his wife and three children. In 1910, he died at age 74.

The Mark Twain house in Hartford is beautifully maintained and open to visitors. See **http://www.marktwainhouse.org/** for more information.

Possible Texts for Text Comparisons

Consider having students read *The Adventures of Tom Sawyer, Detective*, narrated by Huck Finn, who describes their adventures and misadventures during a river trip. Huck, Tom, and Jim drift away from home on a raft in *The Adventures of Huckleberry Finn*. In *Tom Sawyer, Abroad*, Tom sails across the Atlantic with Huck and Jim, having more adventures along the way. For comparison to another book by Mark Twain, consider *The Prince and the Pauper* or *A Connecticut Yankee in King Arthur's Court*.

Book Summary of *The Adventures of Tom Sawyer*

Tom Sawyer may be one of the most vexing and charming characters in literary history. From the time he wakes up in the morning until the time he goes to bed, he expends most of his considerable energy in making, escaping, or instigating trouble. Fortunately for Tom, he is also lovable, and his guardian, Aunt Polly, strives to dispense discipline with an equal dose of affection.

For Tom, life is one long adventure. He manages to convince some of his friends that whitewashing a fence is a privilege worth paying for. He charms and annoys, in turn, the pretty new girl in town, Becky Thatcher. On one misadventure, Tom and his friends Huck Finn and Joe Harper witness a murder, which the boys swear to keep secret out of fear of retribution.

The three friends decide to leave town, pretending to be pirates on a nearby island, while the town assumes they have drowned. Tom, sneaking back to leave a message that they are safe, discovers the unfolding drama surrounding their disappearance, and the friends decide to sneak into their own funerals. Their appearance is greeted with great relief and joy by the townspeople.

During the murder trial of the wrongly accused town drunk, Tom testifies that Injun Joe is the actual murderer. To Tom's dismay, Injun Joe escapes. Despite the threat of retribution, Tom and Huck decide to go in search of treasure, sidetracked by a picnic organized by Becky. Tom and Becky get lost in a cave and are stranded for several days. They eventually escape, thanks to Tom's persistence. In short order, the cave is closed down, trapping Injun Joe, who starves to death. Tom and Huck recover a real treasure to the amazement of the town members, and their adventures come to a close—for the moment.

Note: Mark Twain's writing is consistent with the time in which it was written, the late 1800s. There is considerable dialect and contrived spellings, which may present reading challenges. The book has been challenged because it includes profanity, smoking, and racism. After you preread the book, you may consider these options: proceed with the use of the book; read the book aloud, modifying the text as necessary; or having parents sign a waiver stating that they understand that this classic book includes some content that may be considered objectionable.

Cross-Curricular Connection

This book is appropriate for social studies, literary criticism, and literature studies.

Possible Texts for Text Sets
- Defoe, Daniel. *Robinson Crusoe*. Dover, 1998.
- Green, Roger Lancelyn. *The Adventures of Robin Hood*. Puffin, 2010.
- Swift, Jonathan. *Gulliver's Travels*. Dover, 2012.
- Verne, Jules. *Around the World in Eighty Days*. Dover, 2000.

Name _____

Date _____

Pre-Reading Theme Thoughts

Directions: Read each of the statements in the first column. Decide if you agree or disagree with the statements. Record your opinion by marking an X in Agree or Disagree for each statement. Explain your choices in the fourth column. There are no right or wrong answers.

Statement	Agree	Disagree	Explain Your Answer
It is okay to trick other people into doing your chores if they think they are having fun.			
Running away can be a grand adventure.			
It is okay to keep a secret if you think you are in danger.			
Lying is okay if it helps out a friend.			

Vocabulary Overview

Ten key words from this section are provided below with definitions and sentences about how the words are used in the book. Choose one of the vocabulary activity sheets (pages 15 or 16) for students to complete as they read this section. Monitor students as they work to ensure the definitions they have found are accurate and relate to the text. Finally, discuss these important vocabulary words with students. If you think these words or other words in the section warrant more time devoted to them, there are suggestions in the introduction for other vocabulary activities (page 5).

Word	Definition	Sentence about Text
peril (ch. 1)	danger; something that is likely to cause injury, pain, or harm	Tom believes that he is in great **peril** when Aunt Polly raises the switch.
diligence (ch. 1)	persistence; effort	Tom's **diligence** pays off, and he becomes good at whistling.
alacrity (ch. 2)	eagerness; cheerful readiness	Tom is happy to have help with whitewashing, and he gives up the brush with **alacrity**.
exhibit (ch. 3)	to show; to make available for people to see	Tom watches for Becky, but she doesn't **exhibit** herself again.
audacious (ch. 3)	daring; bold and surprising	Aunt Polly knows that Tom can rarely resist getting into **audacious** mischief.
disconcerted (ch. 4)	unsettled; thrown into confusion	Tom, who avoids being clean, is **disconcerted** at the thought of a good scrubbing.
facetious (ch. 5)	silly; foolish	The serious parson rarely says anything **facetious**.
fetters (ch. 6)	shackles; chains	For Tom, going to school feels like being in jail with **fetters** around his ankles.
pariah (ch. 6)	outsider; someone who is despised and rejected by other people	Huck Finn is so lazy and rude that he is made a **pariah** in the village.
upbraids (ch. 7)	scolds; speaks in an angry or critical way	Becky is so upset that she cries and **upbraids** herself for being mean to Tom.

Name

Date

Understanding Vocabulary Words

Directions: The following words appear in this section of the book. Use context clues and reference materials to determine an accurate definition for each word.

Word	Definition
peril (ch. 1)	
diligence (ch. 1)	
alacrity (ch. 2)	
exhibit (ch. 3)	
audacious (ch. 3)	
disconcerted (ch. 4)	
facetious (ch. 5)	
fetters (ch. 6)	
pariah (ch. 6)	
upbraids (ch. 7)	

Name _____

Date _____

During-Reading Vocabulary Activity

Directions: As you read these chapters, record at least eight important words on the lines below. Try to find interesting, difficult, intriguing, special, or funny words. Your words can be long or short. They can be hard or easy to spell. After each word, use context clues in the text and reference materials to define the word.

- _____
- _____
- _____
- _____
- _____
- _____
- _____
- _____
- _____
- _____

Directions: Respond to these questions about the words in this section.

1. Tom feels great **melancholy** when he looks at the fence that he needs to whitewash. Describe why he feels that way.

   _____

   _____

2. Sid gets into lots of mischief, but he seems to have **immunity** from punishment. Do you think this is fair? Why or why not?

   _____

   _____

Analyzing the Literature

Provided below are discussion questions you can use in small groups, with the whole class, or for written assignments. Each question is given at two levels so you can choose the right question for each group of students. Activity sheets with these questions are provided (pages 18–19) if you want students to write their responses. For each question, a few key discussion points are provided for your reference.

Story Element	■ Level 1	▲ Level 2	Key Discussion Points
Character	Would you want Tom as a friend? Why or why not?	Compare the characters of Tom and Sid. Who would you prefer as a brother? Why?	Opinions may vary, but students may consider that Tom is mischievous but good-hearted, and Sid is better behaved but also willing to let Tom take the blame when he breaks the sugar bowl. Discuss how siblings can have mixed emotions toward each other. Use Tom and Sid as examples.
Plot	How does Tom get help with the whitewashing of the fence?	Do you think Tom is justified in getting his friends to help with the fence? Would you fall for the trick? Why or why not?	Tom pretends to like painting so others will want to try it. He uses his wits to get a tough job done quickly and without much effort on his part. His ability to convince his friends to do chores for fun shows how mischievous, but also clever, Tom is.
Setting	Describe both the inside and outside of the schoolhouse.	How is the schoolhouse similar to and different from your school?	The schoolhouse is small. The students sit on pine benches, while the master sits in an armchair. The children play outside during recess. Some go home for lunch. There is no mention of a playground or playground equipment.
Plot	How does Tom manage to get a Bible?	Why do you think Tom wants to have a Bible when he doesn't like memorizing verses? How do you think people react to his saying that David and Goliath were disciples?	Tom trades various items for the tickets needed to get a Bible. He likes the attention and honor associated with getting one. People probably laugh at his mistake, and many probably realize that something is fishy about the situation.

Name _____

Date _____

Analyzing the Literature

Directions: Think about the section you just read. Read each question and state your response with textual evidence.

1. Would you want Tom as a friend? Why or why not?

_____

_____

_____

_____

2. How does Tom get help with the whitewashing of the fence?

_____

_____

_____

_____

3. Describe the both the inside and outside of the schoolhouse.

_____

_____

_____

_____

4. How does Tom manage to get a Bible?

_____

_____

_____

_____

Name _____

Date _____

▲ Analyzing the Literature

Directions: Think about the section you just read. Read each question and state your response with textual evidence.

1. Compare the characters of Tom and Sid. Who would you prefer as a brother? Why?

_____

_____

_____

_____

2. Do you think Tom is justified in getting his friends to help with the fence? Would you fall for the trick? Why or why not?

_____

_____

_____

_____

3. How is the schoolhouse similar to and different from your school?

_____

_____

_____

4. Why do you think Tom wants to have a Bible when he doesn't like memorizing verses? How do you think people react to his saying that David and Goliath were disciples?

_____

_____

_____

Name _____

Date _____

Reader Response

Directions: Choose one of the following prompts about this section to answer. Be sure you include a topic sentence in your response, use textual evidence to support your opinion, and provide a strong conclusion that summarizes your opinion.

Writing Prompts

- **Opinion/Argument Piece**—If you knew Becky, would you encourage her to try to win back Tom's affections? If so, what do you think she should do? If you think she should not try to win him back, explain why.
- **Informative/Explanatory Piece**—In chapter 8, Tom states several incantations. *Incantations* are chants or sayings. They show how superstitious he is. Find and describe two or three of his incantations in the story. Explain why they can't really work.

_____

_____

_____

_____

_____

_____

_____

_____

_____

_____

_____

_____

_____

Name _____

Date _____

Close Reading the Literature

Directions: Closely reread the first two paragraphs of chapter 7. Read each question and then revisit the text to find evidence that supports your answer.

1. Use text evidence to describe what helps cause Tom's boredom.

   _____

   _____

   _____

2. What does Cardiff Hill look like? Use descriptive examples in the text to support your answer.

   _____

   _____

   _____

3. Explain why the tick has no reason to be happy about being let out of the box.

   _____

   _____

   _____

4. Find an example of cause and effect based on the events in the second paragraph.

   _____

   _____

   _____

Name _____

Date _____

Making Connections—Using Your Senses

Directions: Mark Twain grew up in Missouri near the Mississippi River. He writes so that you can see, taste, smell, feel, and hear the story. Choose a setting from this section, such as the school, church, or woods. Describe what is happening in that part of the story using each of the five senses.

Setting/ Location	
What I See	
What I Taste	
What I Smell	
What I Feel	
What I Hear	

1. Mark Twain uses a lot of humor when writing about Tom. Write one example of how Tom makes you smile.

   _____

   _____

   _____

© Shell Education

Name

Date

Creating with the Story Elements

Directions: Thinking about the story elements of character, setting, and plot in a novel is very important to understanding what is happening and why. Complete **one** of the following activities based on what you've read so far. Be creative and have fun!

Characters

People sometimes say that opposites attract. Make a chart like the one below that shows how Becky and Tom can be considered opposites.

Becky	Tom
•	•
•	•
•	•

Setting

Use reference books or the Internet to find pictures of a 19th century one-room schoolhouse. Make a diorama or detailed drawing of what Tom's schoolhouse might look like.

Plot

Tom and Joe think it would be great to be outlaws for a year in Sherwood Forest. Make a list of at least ten things they should pack in order to survive for a week in the forest.

Vocabulary Overview

Ten key words from this section are provided below with definitions and sentences about how the words are used in the book. Choose one of the vocabulary activity sheets (pages 25 or 26) for students to complete as they read this section. Monitor students as they work to ensure the definitions they have found are accurate and relate to the text. Finally, discuss these important vocabulary words with students. If you think these words or other words in the section warrant more time devoted to them, there are suggestions in the introduction for other vocabulary activities (page 5).

Word	Definition	Sentence about Text
monotonous (ch. 9)	dull; boring	Listening to the men dig for such a long time is **monotonous** for Tom and Huck.
ingenuity (ch. 9)	skill; cleverness that allows someone to solve problems	It would take great **ingenuity** to figure out where the chirping cricket is hiding.
caterwauling (ch. 9)	yowling; loud and unpleasant sound	Tom hears the **caterwauling** of a cat in the night.
faze (ch. 10)	disturb; upset	Nothing **fazes** Muff Potter, not even getting a whack on the head.
culprit (ch. 10)	person who has committed a crime or done something wrong	Tom expects to be found out as the **culprit** and is ready for punishment.
perplexed (ch. 11)	puzzled; unable to understand something clearly	Tom looks **perplexed** and confused when Muff Potter is arrested.
newfangled (ch. 12)	modern; of the newest style or kind	Tom seems so dull that Aunt Polly tries out **newfangled** medicine on him.
succumb (ch. 13)	give in; stop trying to resist something	Becky tells Tom to leave, and he feels that he has to **succumb** to her wishes.
sumptuous (ch. 15)	splendid; very expensive or impressive	The breakfast of bacon and fresh fish makes a **sumptuous** feast for the boys.
ominous (ch. 16)	gloomy; suggestion that something bad is going to happen	The silence becomes **ominous** as Tom and Huck watch Joe get ready to leave.

Name _____

Date _____

Understanding Vocabulary Words

Directions: The following words appear in this section of the book. Use context clues and reference materials to determine an accurate definition for each word.

Word	Definition
monotonous (ch. 9)	
ingenuity (ch. 9)	
caterwauling (ch. 9)	
faze (ch. 10)	
culprit (ch. 10)	
perplexed (ch. 11)	
newfangled (ch. 12)	
succumb (ch. 13)	
sumptuous (ch. 15)	
ominous (ch. 16)	

Name _____

Date _____

During-Reading Vocabulary Activity

Directions: As you read these chapters, record at least eight important words on the lines below. Try to find interesting, difficult, intriguing, special, or funny words. Your words can be long or short. They can be hard or easy to spell. After each word, use context clues in the text and reference materials to define the word.

- _____
- _____
- _____
- _____
- _____
- _____
- _____
- _____
- _____
- _____

Directions: Respond to these questions about the words in this section.

1. Why are the boys **jubilant** when they realize people think they have drowned?

_____

_____

2. During the funeral for the boys, the minister tells a **pathetic** tale of the drowned boys. Why is the tale described as **pathetic**?

_____

_____

Analyzing the Literature

Provided below are discussion questions you can use in small groups, with the whole class, or for written assignments. Each question is given at two levels so you can choose the right question for each group of students. Activity sheets with these questions are provided (pages 28–29) if you want students to write their responses. For each question, a few key discussion points are provided for your reference.

Story Element	■ Level 1	▲ Level 2	Key Discussion Points
Setting	Describe what the graveyard looks like.	Mark Twain describes the graveyard as an old-fashioned, western kind. How would that compare to a modern graveyard?	The graveyard is on a hill with a "crazy" board fence, grass and weeds, sunken graves, and boards for markers. A modern graveyard would have well-tended gardens, permanent markers, sculptures, or even mausoleums.
Plot	Why do you think the three men are digging up a grave? What might they find?	Why do the men who are digging up the grave argue? What grudge does Injun Joe have?	The men probably hope to find something valuable, such as a wedding ring or other belongings. They argue over payment, and Injun Joe is angry because the doctor didn't help him out years before.
Character	Do you think Tom and Huck are brave or simply foolish? Why?	Mark Twain says that Tom and Huck have the spirit of adventure. Give examples to show how they are adventurous.	Tom and Huck are willing to go to a graveyard, and they later go to the island. Tom is willing to risk sneaking back home at night. They show some courage. However, they are also superstitious and fearful at times, and they make some foolish choices.
Plot	How do people react to the boys showing up at their funeral?	Aunt Polly alternates between cuffing and kissing Tom after the funeral. Why does she do both?	The people are relieved and excited. They are so happy to see the boys that they aren't terribly upset about being misled. Aunt Polly is exasperated with Tom, but she's also very happy to have him safely home.

Name _____

Date _____

Analyzing the Literature

Directions: Think about the section you just read. Read each question and state your response with textual evidence.

1. Describe what the graveyard looks like.

   _____

   _____

   _____

   _____

2. Why do you think the three men are digging up a grave? What might they find?

   _____

   _____

   _____

   _____

3. Do you think Tom and Huck are brave or simply foolish? Why?

   _____

   _____

   _____

   _____

4. How do people react to the boys showing up at their funeral?

   _____

   _____

   _____

   _____

Name _____

Date _____

▲ Analyzing the Literature

Directions: Think about the section you just read. Read each question and state your response with textual evidence.

1. Mark Twain describes the graveyard as an old-fashioned, western kind. How would that compare to a modern graveyard?

_____

_____

_____

_____

2. Why do the men who are digging up the grave argue? What grudge does Injun Joe have?

_____

_____

_____

_____

3. Mark Twain says that Tom and Huck have the spirit of adventure. Give examples to show how they are adventurous.

_____

_____

_____

4. Aunt Polly alternates between cuffing and kissing Tom after the funeral. Why does she do both?

_____

_____

_____

Name _____

Date _____

Reader Response

Directions: Choose one of the following prompts about this section to answer. Be sure you include a topic sentence in your response, use textual evidence to support your opinion, and provide a strong conclusion that summarizes your opinion.

Writing Prompts

- **Informative/Explanatory Piece**—Compare the graveyard in Tom's village to one in or near your community. Include at least two examples that support your comparison.
- **Opinion/Argument Piece**—Think about how the boys fear Injun Joe. What events led up to their fear? Do you think the boys are obligated to tell the truth about why they ran away, even if it puts them at risk? Or should they wait to see what happens and hope that the truth comes out anyway?

_____

_____

_____

_____

_____

_____

_____

_____

_____

_____

_____

_____

_____

_____

Close Reading the Literature

Directions: Closely reread the first two paragraphs of chapter 14. Read each question and then revisit the text to find evidence that supports your answer.

1. Use text details to explain what Tom sees when he wakes up.

   _____

   _____

   _____

2. Tom is very superstitious. Find an example of one of his superstitions.

   _____

   _____

   _____

3. What text clues tell you that this would be a good place to go bird watching?

   _____

   _____

   _____

4. Explain why the "fox" squirrel approaches the boys. Use the description to support your answer.

   _____

   _____

   _____

   _____

Name _____

Date _____

Making Connections–Groceries in the 1880s

Directions: Most people don't make a lot of money in Tom's village. A fireman makes about $1.60 per day. However, things don't cost a lot either. A pair of jeans costs about $1.25. Review the prices of the following grocery items. Choose at least five things to buy for a good meal. Then, use the newspaper or online advertisements to determine today's costs. Write those in the fourth column. Find the totals and compare the prices.

Grocery Items	Quantity	1880s Prices	Current Prices
1 pound of bacon		13 cents	
1 pound of pork chops		11 cents	
1 pound of butter		26 cents	
½ gallon of milk		14 cents	
1 pound of coffee		25 cents	
10 pounds of potatoes		16 cents	
1 orange		3 cents	
1 jar of marmalade		25 cents	
1 dozen eggs		21 cents	
1 can of tomatoes		15 cents	
1 pound of spaghetti		16 cents	
1 pound of cheese		18 cents	
5 pounds of sugar		35 cents	
	Totals		

Name _____

Date _____

Creating with the Story Elements

Directions: Thinking about the story elements of character, setting, and plot in a novel is very important to understanding what is happening and why. Complete **one** of the following activities based on what you've read so far. Be creative and have fun!

Characters

Huck doesn't attend school. However, he has what might be called "street smarts." Create a report card that grades Huck on his actions in this section. Choose at least three characteristics to grade (courage, tenacity, etc.). Justify each grade.

Setting

Draw a picture or create a map that shows an ideal campsite. Get ideas from the story and add features that you would want. Include labels that identify the key features of your campsite.

Plot

Think about what might happen next if the boys decide to go to the police instead of running away. Think about whether they'd be believed, what Injun Joe might do, and how other characters would react. Create a plot outline with your choices.

Vocabulary Overview

Ten key words from this section are provided below with definitions and sentences about how the words are used in the book. Choose one of the vocabulary activity sheets (pages 35 or 36) for students to complete as they read this section. Monitor students as they work to ensure the definitions they have found are accurate and relate to the text. Finally, discuss these important vocabulary words with students. If you think these words or other words in the section warrant more time devoted to them, there are suggestions in the introduction for other vocabulary activities (page 5).

Word	Definition	Sentence about Text
wistfully (ch. 18)	longingly; having or showing sad thoughts or feelings about something that you want	Aunt Polly says **wistfully** that she wishes Tom had told her that he was safe.
repentant (ch. 18)	regretful; sorry	Tom feels **repentant** about making Aunt Polly worry so much about him.
trounce (ch. 20)	beat; thrash	Tom can't **trounce** a girl like he might a boy that he's mad at.
vexation (ch. 20)	annoyance	Becky is so upset that she cries with **vexation**.
folly (ch. 20)	foolishness; lack of good sense or judgment	When Tom admits to a misdeed, the class is amazed at his **folly**.
treachery (ch. 20)	disloyalty; act of being disloyal to someone who trusts you	Becky tells how she has wronged Tom, admitting to her **treachery**.
dignitaries (ch. 21)	important people; people of high rank or important positions	The mayor is one of the town's **dignitaries**.
fluctuating (ch. 22)	changing; to change or shift uncertainly	Tom worries about the judge's **fluctuating** condition, wishing he could trust what was likely to happen.
mesmerizer (ch. 22)	a person who hypnotizes	Seeing a **mesmerizer** hypnotize people at the circus is very entertaining to Tom.
endurance (ch. 22)	strength; ability to withstand hardship	Tom is not sure that he has the **endurance** to live through the terrible thunderstorm.

Name _____

Date _____

Understanding Vocabulary Words

Directions: The following words appear in this section of the book. Use context clues and reference materials to determine an accurate definition for each word.

Word	Definition
wistfully (ch. 18)	
repentant (ch. 18)	
trounce (ch. 20)	
vexation (ch. 20)	
folly (ch. 20)	
treachery (ch. 20)	
dignitaries (ch. 21)	
fluctuating (ch. 22)	
mesmerizer (ch. 22)	
endurance (ch. 22)	

Name _____

Date _____

During-Reading Vocabulary Activity

Directions: As you read these chapters, record at least eight important words on the lines below. Try to find interesting, difficult, intriguing, special, or funny words. Your words can be long or short. They can be hard or easy to spell. After each word, use context clues in the text and reference materials to define the word.

- _____
- _____
- _____
- _____
- _____
- _____
- _____
- _____
- _____
- _____

Directions: Now, organize your words. Rewrite each of your words on a sticky note. Work as a group to create a bar graph of your words. You should stack any words that are the same on top of one another. Different words appear in different columns. Finally, discuss with a group why certain words were chosen more often than other words.

Analyzing the Literature

Provided below are discussion questions you can use in small groups, with the whole class, or for written assignments. Each question is given at two levels so you can choose the right question for each group of students. Activity sheets with these questions are provided (pages 38–39) if you want students to write their responses. For each question, a few key discussion points are provided for your reference.

Story Element	■ Level 1	▲ Level 2	Key Discussion Points
Plot	Describe the dream that Tom lies about when talking with Aunt Polly and Mary in chapter 18.	Why does Tom lie about the dream in chapter 18? How is he found out? What makes Aunt Polly feel better about his lie?	Tom wants to make Aunt Polly feel better about not telling her that he was alive, so he describes what he saw when he snuck off the island as if it were a dream. When Aunt Polly learns that he sneaked back, she is angry with him for lying to her. She feels better when she finds the bark with Tom's note on it in his pocket.
Character	What does Tom do in school that finally wins back Becky Thatcher's affections?	What is Tom's punishment for claiming that he tore the book? Do you think it would be worth it to you if you had that choice?	Tom says he tore the teacher's book (to protect Becky) and is lashed by the teacher. Becky tells him that he is noble for doing such a thing. Though opinions will differ as to whether it would be worth the lashing, consider the time in which the book was written. Discuss the practice of corporal punishment in schools in the past.
Plot	Describe the prank that the students play on the schoolmaster in chapter 21.	Do you think the schoolmaster deserves to be pranked in chapter 21? Why or why not?	The schoolmaster's bald head is gilded with gold paint during his early nap, and a cat is suspended so that it pulls off his wig. Opinions will vary on whether or not the schoolmaster deserves to be pranked. Consider the schoolmaster's severity against the embarrassment he experiences.
Setting	Describe the activities in the town that keep Tom entertained in chapter 22 until he gets the measles.	Compare the summer activities of Tom's town with the summer activities in your town. How are they alike and different?	During the summer, Judge Frazer passes away, and there is a funeral held for him; Tom and Joe Harper go to the minstrel show; the circus comes to town for three days; and there are some "boys-and-girls' parties." Compare to similar town/city events today.

Name _____

Date _____

Analyzing the Literature

Directions: Think about the section you just read. Read each question and state your response with textual evidence.

1. Describe the dream that Tom lies about when talking with Aunt Polly and Mary in chapter 18.

_____

_____

_____

_____

2. What does Tom do in school that finally wins back Becky Thatcher's affections?

_____

_____

_____

_____

3. Describe the prank that the students play on the schoolmaster in chapter 21.

_____

_____

_____

_____

4. Describe the activities in the town that keep Tom entertained in chapter 22 until he gets the measles.

_____

_____

_____

▲ Analyzing the Literature

Directions: Think about the section you just read. Read each question and state your response with textual evidence.

1. Why does Tom lie about the dream in chapter 18? How is he found out? What makes Aunt Polly feel better about his lie?

_____

_____

_____

_____

2. What is Tom's punishment for claiming that he tore the book? Do you think it would be worth it to you if you had that choice?

_____

_____

_____

_____

3. Do you think the schoolmaster deserves to be pranked in chapter 21? Why or why not?

_____

_____

_____

4. Compare the summer activities of Tom's town with the summer activities in your town. How are they alike and different?

_____

_____

_____

Name

Date

Reader Response

Directions: Choose one of the following prompts about this section to answer. Be sure you include a topic sentence in your response, use textual evidence to support your opinion, and provide a strong conclusion that summarizes your opinion.

Writing Prompts

- **Opinion/Argument Piece**—Do you think it is okay to punish students like Tom with lashings? Consider the time in which the story takes place, Tom's frequent misbehaviors, whether physical punishments are ever justified, and so forth.
- **Narrative Piece**—Describe two contrasting reactions that the schoolmaster could have to the prank. Then, describe how you think he would react.

Close Reading the Literature

Directions: Closely reread the first paragraph of chapter 21. Read each question and then revisit the text to find evidence that supports your answer.

1. Which students escape the lashings? Why do you think they do? Use the text to support your answer with what you've learned about the schoolmaster.

   _____

   _____

   _____

2. Describe the schoolmaster's appearance, giving two examples from the text.

   _____

   _____

   _____

3. What reason is given in the book for the sign painter's son wanting to help with the prank?

   _____

   _____

4. What helps ensure that the boys can carry out their plan? Find at least two conditions in the paragraph.

   _____

   _____

   _____

Name _____

Date _____

Making Connections—Tom's Dilemma

Directions: Tom struggles between being good and being naughty many times throughout the book. This kind of problem is called a *dilemma*. Choose one dilemma Tom experiences in this section. In the chart, describe the attractions of being good and the attractions of being naughty. Then, answer the questions.

Tom's dilemma: _____

The Attractions of Being Good	The Attractions of Being Naughty

Which does Tom choose? _____

What are the main reasons for his choice?

_____

_____

Creating with the Story Elements

Directions: Thinking about the story elements of character, setting, and plot in a novel is very important to understanding what is happening and why. Complete **one** of the following activities based on what you've read so far. Be creative and have fun!

Characters

Which character do you like the *least* so far? Create a list of your complaints about the character. Include characteristics such as behavior, attitude, thoughts, and appearance.

Setting

Create a chart that contrasts Tom's small village with where you live today. Think about features such as kinds of homes, businesses, modes of transportation, schools, activities, geographical features, and so forth.

Plot

Make a story map of the key events of the story so far. Once you have mapped through chapter 22, give three possible predictions for the next events.

Vocabulary Overview

Ten key words from this section are provided below with definitions and sentences about how the words are used in the book. Choose one of the vocabulary activity sheets (pages 45 or 46) for students to complete as they read this section. Monitor students as they work to ensure the definitions they have found are accurate and relate to the text. Finally, discuss these important vocabulary words with students. If you think these words or other words in the section warrant more time devoted to them, there are suggestions in the introduction for other vocabulary activities (page 5).

Word	Definition	Sentence about Text
stolid (ch. 23)	indifferent; showing little or no emotion	Injun Joe seems **stolid** in the courtroom, sitting as if nothing matters.
depose (ch. 23)	give a sworn statement	A lawyer may **depose** a witness, asking questions about what they know about a crime.
contemptuous (ch. 23)	scornful; feeling or showing deep disapproval	Injun Joe can't help feeling disdainful and **contemptuous** about the trial.
enterprise (ch. 24)	an activity or project that is often difficult	Huck thinks that hunting for treasure is a great **enterprise**.
unkempt (ch. 26)	rumpled; not neat or orderly; messy	The stranger looks shabby and **unkempt**.
infernal (ch. 26)	very bad or unpleasant	The men blame the **infernal** boys for being in the way of their plans.
gloating (ch. 26)	joyful thinking about something with triumph or delight	The boys cannot help **gloating** when they see the money.
contemplate (ch. 26)	consider; think deeply about something	The men think about the future while they **contemplate** the treasure.
ostentatious (ch. 27)	flashy; displaying wealth in a way that's meant to attract attention	The **ostentatious** house is much more grand than Aunt Polly's house.
auspicious (ch. 28)	promising; suggesting that future success is likely	The dark, quiet night gives the fortunate boys an **auspicious** start to their adventure.

Name

Date

Understanding Vocabulary Words

Directions: The following words appear in this section of the book. Use context clues and reference materials to determine an accurate definition for each word.

Word	Definition
stolid (ch. 23)	
depose (ch. 23)	
contemptuous (ch. 23)	
enterprise (ch. 24)	
unkempt (ch. 26)	
infernal (ch. 26)	
gloating (ch. 26)	
contemplate (ch. 26)	
ostentatious (ch. 27)	
auspicious (ch. 28)	

Name _____

Date _____

During-Reading Vocabulary Activity

Directions: As you read these chapters, record at least eight important words on the lines below. Try to find interesting, difficult, intriguing, special, or funny words. Your words can be long or short. They can be hard or easy to spell. After each word, use context clues in the text and reference materials to define the word.

- _____

- _____

- _____

- _____

- _____

- _____

- _____

- _____

- _____

- _____

Directions: Respond to these questions about the words in this section.

1. At the end of chapter 25, the boys give the haunted house a **wide berth**. What does "giving a **wide berth**" mean? Why do they do that?

   _____

   _____

2. In chapter 26, the haunted house is said to be depressing because of the **desolation**. What is it about the house that makes it seem this way?

   _____

   _____

Analyzing the Literature

Provided below are discussion questions you can use in small groups, with the whole class, or for written assignments. Each question is given at two levels so you can choose the right question for each group of students. Activity sheets with these questions are provided (pages 48–49) if you want students to write their responses. For each question, a few key discussion points are provided for your reference.

Story Element	■ Level 1	▲ Level 2	Key Discussion Points
Plot	Why do the people of the town consider Tom to be a hero again?	After the trial, Tom has conflicting feelings about the outcome. Why?	Tom is a hero because he ensures that Injun Joe doesn't get away with murder and that Muff Potter is freed. He enjoys being praised and admired. However, he is also terribly worried that Injun Joe, even if captured, will seek his revenge on Tom.
Setting	What saves Tom and Huck from being found by the men in the haunted house?	Why do you think Mark Twain includes a haunted house as part of the setting?	The staircase gives out when Injun Joe starts upstairs, and he gives up. Mark Twain may have added a haunted house because it's a useful place for hiding treasure, it's intriguing as a story setting, and kids like to explore haunted houses.
Character	Do you think Injun Joe will kill the boys if he catches them? Why or why not?	Tom thinks that it is small comfort to be the only one in danger from Injun Joe. What does he mean? Do you think Injun Joe will seek revenge on Huck, too? Why or why not?	Opinions may vary on Injun Joe's level of anger at Tom and whether he will hurt both boys. This may be a good opportunity to discuss the choice of Injun Joe as such a despicable character and the implicit racism in the choice.
Plot	Why don't Huck and Tom go back to the tavern to look for the box after Tom finds Injun Joe asleep?	What is it about the Temperance Taverns that troubles Tom and Huck?	Injun Joe is asleep due to drinking, but he appears not to be drunk enough for them to safely return. The Temperance Taverns have barrels and bottles of whiskey in the back room. The boys think the rooms are "haunted" with whiskey.

Name _____

Date _____

Analyzing the Literature

Directions: Think about the section you just read. Read each question and state your response with textual evidence.

1. Why do the people of the town consider Tom to be a hero again?

_____

_____

_____

_____

2. What saves Tom and Huck from being found by the men in the haunted house?

_____

_____

_____

_____

3. Do you think Injun Joe will kill the boys if he catches them? Why or why not?

_____

_____

_____

_____

4. Why don't Huck and Tom go back to the tavern to look for the box after Tom finds Injun Joe asleep?

_____

_____

_____

Name _____

Date _____

▲ Analyzing the Literature

Directions: Think about the section you just read. Read each question and state your response with textual evidence.

1. After the trial, Tom has conflicting feelings about the outcome. Why?

_____

_____

_____

_____

2. Why do you think Mark Twain includes a haunted house as part of the setting?

_____

_____

_____

_____

3. Tom thinks that it is small comfort to be the only one in danger from Injun Joe. What does he mean? Do you think Injun Joe will seek revenge on Huck, too? Why or why not?

_____

_____

_____

_____

4. What is it about the Temperance Taverns that troubles Tom and Huck?

_____

_____

_____

Name _____

Date _____

Reader Response

Directions: Choose one of the following prompts about this section to answer. Be sure you include a topic sentence in your response, use textual evidence to support your opinion, and provide a strong conclusion that summarizes your opinion.

Writing Prompts

- **Opinion/Argument Piece**—Think about Tom and Huck's plan as described at the end of chapter 28. If you were in their position, what plan would you make? How is it similar to and different from their plan?
- **Narrative Piece**—Huck lives on his own. Describe how Mark Twain's choice to have this character live alone contributes to the plot of the story. Give at least three examples drawn from the story.

_____

_____

_____

_____

_____

_____

_____

_____

_____

_____

_____

_____

_____

_____

Name

Date

Close Reading the Literature

Directions: Closely reread the first two paragraphs of chapter 27. Read each question and then revisit the text to find evidence that supports your answer.

1. Describe how Tom feels about his dreams as he first wakes up in the morning. Include where and when they seem to happen.

     _____

     _____

     _____

2. What tells you that finding thousands of dollars is hard for Tom to imagine?

     _____

     _____

     _____

3. What does Tom think of as a typical treasure? Give examples from the text, and think about what he has saved or found before.

     _____

     _____

     _____

4. Why does Tom go to see Huck? Use text evidence to form your conclusion.

     _____

     _____

     _____

Name _____

Date _____

Making Connections—Character Checklist

Directions: Choose a character from the story and consider how he or she behaves. Then, use what you know about the character to fill in the chart. Read each characteristic and indicate with an *x* if the character acts that way: always, sometimes, or never.

Your character: _____

Behavior	Always	Sometimes	Never
friendly			
shy			
clever			
mean			
funny			
adventurous			
likeable			
impulsive			

Choose two characteristics that best fit your character. Explain your choices.

_____

_____

_____

_____

Name _____

Date _____

Creating with the Story Elements

Directions: Thinking about the story elements of character, setting, and plot in a novel is very important to understanding what is happening and why. Complete **one** of the following activities based on what you've read so far. Be creative and have fun!

Characters

Create a wanted poster for Injun Joe. Describe why he is wanted, include a reward, and describe what he looks like.

Setting

Design a floor plan for the haunted house based on the description in chapter 26. Or create a drawing of the exterior of the house based on the description in chapter 25.

Plot

A horoscope gives advice or predicts the future. Based on what you know about Injun Joe, write a horoscope that would help guide him in his future choices.

Vocabulary Overview

Ten key words from this section are provided below with definitions and sentences about how the words are used in the book. Choose one of the vocabulary activity sheets (pages 55 or 56) for students to complete as they read this section. Monitor students as they work to ensure the definitions they have found are accurate and relate to the text. Finally, discuss these important vocabulary words with students. If you think these words or other words in the section warrant more time devoted to them, there are suggestions in the introduction for other vocabulary activities (page 5).

Word	Definition	Sentence about Text
hospitality (ch. 29)	kindness; generous and friendly treatment of visitors or guests	Widow Douglas's **hospitality** is tempting, especially since she always has ice cream.
labyrinth (ch. 29)	maze; a place with many confusing passages or paths	The cave is a **labyrinth** of pathways, much like a web.
embellishment (ch. 30)	exaggeration	The story isn't exactly a lie. It's more like an **embellishment**.
preservation (ch. 30)	protection; prevention of harm or loss	The widow feels grateful for her defense and **preservation**.
fugitives (ch. 31)	runaways trying to avoid being captured	When the bats fly at them, the children become **fugitives** as they try to escape.
profound (ch. 31)	intense; very strongly felt	The silence is so **profound** in the cave that the children can hear their own breathing.
apathy (ch. 31)	indifference; not having much emotion or interest	Becky is so tired that she droops and falls into total **apathy**.
forlorn (ch. 32)	sad; empty and lonely	Aunt Polly is **forlorn**, fearing the worst.
abounding (ch. 33)	abundant; copiously supplied	Tom feels an **abounding** sense of relief when he sees the body.
ransacked (ch. 35)	raided; searched thoroughly	The **ransacked** house has nothing left to rob.

Name _____

Date _____

Understanding Vocabulary Words

Directions: The following words appear in this section of the book. Use context clues and reference materials to determine an accurate definition for each word.

Word	Definition
hospitality (ch. 29)	
labyrinth (ch. 29)	
embellishment (ch. 30)	
preservation (ch. 30)	
fugitives (ch. 31)	
profound (ch. 31)	
apathy (ch. 31)	
forlorn (ch. 32)	
abounding (ch. 33)	
ransacked (ch. 35)	

Name _____

Date _____

During-Reading Vocabulary Activity

Directions: As you read these chapters, choose five important words from the story. Then, use those five words to complete this word flow chart. On each arrow, write a vocabulary word. In the boxes between the words, explain how the words connect. An example for the words *fugitives* and *ransacked* has been done for you.

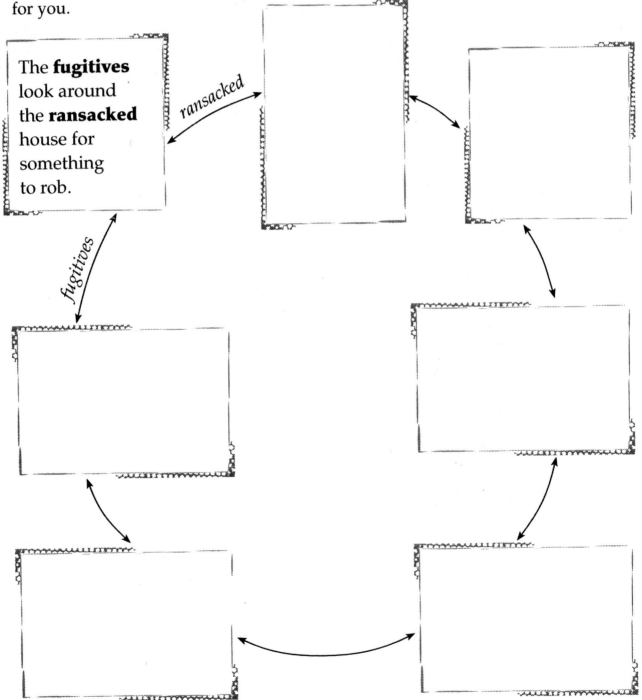

The **fugitives** look around the **ransacked** house for something to rob.

ransacked

fugitives

Analyzing the Literature

Provided below are discussion questions you can use in small groups, with the whole class, or for written assignments. Each question is given at two levels so you can choose the right question for each group of students. Activity sheets with these questions are provided (pages 58–59) if you want students to write their responses. For each question, a few key discussion points are provided for your reference.

Story Element	■ Level 1	▲ Level 2	Key Discussion Points
Character	How does Huck become a hero?	How does Huck show both courage and fear when the Widow Douglas is threatened?	Huck gets help and saves Widow Douglas from Injun Joe and his partners. Huck is brave when he gets help, but he runs away when the shooting starts.
Setting	How do Tom and Becky get lost in the cave?	Describe what Tom and Becky see in the cavern before they realize they are lost.	Tom and Becky startle bats with their candles, and they run when the bats fly at them, causing the two to become lost. They see stalactites, a spring, crystals, and stalagmites all around the cavern.
Plot	How does Tom find the way out of the cave? Why is the time of day important?	How does Tom's personality end up helping them find a way to escape?	Tom uses the kite string from his pocket to try different routes. If it had been at night, he wouldn't have seen the exit. Tom is a persistent problem solver who continues to work through the issue until he solves it.
Plot	What happened to Injun Joe?	Do you think Injun Joe had a just fate? Would it have been better if he'd been caught and brought to trial?	Injun Joe was trapped in the cave and died. Opinions will vary on whether his fate was just, but this question can open up discussions on whether or not "bad guys" are deserving of their fates in this and other texts.

Name _____

Date _____

Analyzing the Literature

Directions: Think about the section you just read. Read each question and state your response with textual evidence.

1. How does Huck become a hero?

   _____

   _____

   _____

   _____

2. How do Tom and Becky get lost in the cave?

   _____

   _____

   _____

   _____

3. How does Tom find the way out of the cave? Why is the time of day important?

   _____

   _____

   _____

   _____

4. What happened to Injun Joe?

   _____

   _____

   _____

   _____

▲ Analyzing the Literature

Directions: Think about the section you just read. Read each question and state your response with textual evidence.

1. How does Huck show both courage and fear when the Widow Douglas is threatened?

_____

_____

_____

_____

2. Describe what Tom and Becky see in the cavern before they realize they are lost.

_____

_____

_____

3. How does Tom's personality end up helping them find a way to escape?

_____

_____

_____

4. Do you think Injun Joe had a just fate? Would it have been better if he'd been caught and brought to trial?

_____

_____

_____

_____

Name _____

Date _____

Reader Response

Directions: Choose one of the following prompts about this section to answer. Be sure you include a topic sentence in your response, use textual evidence to support your opinion, and provide a strong conclusion that summarizes your opinion.

Writing Prompts

- **Opinion/Argument Piece**—Think about what Huck says when he gives Tom his share of the treasure. Knowing Huck from the story, do you think he is right? How would you react to suddenly having lots of money? Do you think it would make you happier?

- **Narrative Piece**—Write about what you think might happen in a sequel to the story. Would Huck leave Widow Douglas? Would he and Tom have more adventures? Give a summary of your sequel, making sure that it fits with the style of the story.

_____

_____

_____

_____

_____

_____

_____

_____

_____

_____

_____

_____

Close Reading the Literature

Directions: Closely reread the first three paragraphs of chapter 35. Read each question and then revisit the text to find evidence that supports your answer.

1. The citizens are very excited about the money. What can you infer about their lifestyles or levels of income from the passage?

   _____

   _____

   _____

2. Find evidence in the text that shows how people have changed their minds about Tom and Huck.

   _____

   _____

   _____

3. Both Tom and Huck get money each week. Find evidence in the text that shows that this is a lot of money.

   _____

   _____

   _____

4. Using the text, explain reasons why Judge Thatcher has formed such a great opinion of Tom.

   _____

   _____

Name _____

Date _____

Making Connections–Rock Candy Crystals

Research what the inside of a cave looks like with its stalactites, stalagmites, and crystals. Then, follow the directions below to grow your own stalactites, stalagmites, and crystals.

Materials

- a clean, narrow jar
- 1 cup (240 mL) water
- a pan
- a stove or hot plate
- a spoon for stirring
- 2–3 cups (400–600 g) sugar
- food coloring, optional
- a piece of clean string or a wooden skewer
- a pencil or clothespin
- scissors

Procedure

1. With the help of an adult, heat the cup of hot water until it boils.

2. Add sugar and stir so it dissolves. Keep adding sugar until it no longer dissolves.

3. Add food coloring if you wish.

4. Pour the sugar solution into a clean, narrow jar.

5. Tie the string onto the center of the pencil. Cut the string so it is long enough to dangle inside the jar. Place the pencil across the top of the jar to hold the string in place. You can also stand the skewer in the jar, holding it in place with the clothespin across the jar.

6. Leave the jar in a safe place. Watch the crystals grow for the next week.

7. Enjoy your rock candy!

Name _____

Date _____

Creating with the Story Elements

Directions: Thinking about the story elements of character, setting, and plot in a novel is very important to understanding what is happening and why. Complete **one** of the following activities based on what you've read so far. Be creative and have fun!

Characters

Write a newspaper article about either Tom or Huck. Give biographical details about the character. Describe his accomplishments.

Setting

Create a brochure that describes tours of the cave. Use chapter 31 in the text to help you find descriptions of the cave. Use the Internet to help you find ideas on what to include in the tour brochure.

Plot

Make a movie poster that advertises the movie version of the book. Include drawings of the main characters, and write an intriguing tagline. Or you can write the script for a movie trailer instead.

Name _____

Date _____

Post-Reading Theme Thoughts

Directions: Read each of the statements in the first column. Choose a main character from *The Adventures of Tom Sawyer*. Think about that character's point of view. From that character's perspective, decide if the character would agree or disagree with the statements. Record the character's opinion by marking an X in Agree or Disagree for each statement. Explain your choices in the fourth column using text evidence.

Character I Chose: _____

Statement	Agree	Disagree	Explain Your Answer
It is okay to trick other people into doing your chores if they think they are having fun.			
Running away can be a grand adventure.			
It is okay to keep a secret if you think you are in danger.			
Lying is okay if it helps out a friend.			

Name _____

Date _____

Culminating Activity: Keeping Current

Directions: Tom Sawyer is an adventurous and often mischievous boy with an active imagination. What other literary character has similar qualities? Choose a character from another book or story you have read. Use the Venn diagram below to list the similarities and differences between Tom Sawyer and the character you choose.

Tom Sawyer

Similarities

Other Character _____

© Shell Education

#40200—Instructional Guide: The Adventures of Tom Sawyer   65

Name _____

Date _____

Culminating Activity:
Keeping Current (cont.)

Directions: Use the same character that you compared to Tom Sawyer in your Venn diagram on page 65 to complete one of the following activities.

- Imagine the character you chose for your Venn diagram is the protagonist of *The Adventures of Tom Sawyer* instead of Tom. Write about what your character would do in the same situations. (For example, what do you think would happen if Lucy from The Chronicles of Narnia series were stuck in a cave with Becky Thatcher? Do you think Lucy would be able to find a way out like Tom did?)

- Imagine that Tom Sawyer is the protagonist in your other character's book. Would the story be the same, or would Tom change the outcome of things? What adventures do you think Tom would go on, and what kind of trouble do you think he would cause? Use your Venn diagram to consider the two characters' similarities and differences and predict how Tom might alter the other story.

- Write your own adventure featuring Tom Sawyer and the character you chose for your Venn diagram. Create a story in which the characters have to work together using their unique personalities and qualities to solve a problem or face a major conflict.

Name

Date

Comprehension Assessment

Directions: Circle the correct response to each question.

1. What is the meaning of the word *vindictive* as it is used in the book?

    A. repentant

    B. accused

    C. spiteful

    D. weary

2. Which detail from the book best supports your answer to question 1?

    E. "Tom fled home at noon."

    F. "Then Alfred went musing into the deserted schoolhouse."

    G. "Amy's happy prattle became intolerable."

    H. Becky "resolved to let him get whipped . . . and to hate him forever."

3. Write the main idea of the text below in the graphic organizer.

    "Huck Finn's wealth and the fact that he was now under the Widow Douglas' protection introduced him into society—no, dragged him into it, hurled him into it—and his sufferings were almost more than he could bear. The widow's servants kept him clean and neat, combed and brushed, and they bedded him nightly in unsympathetic sheets that had not one little spot or stain which he could press to his heart and know for a friend. He had to eat with knife and fork; he had to use napkin, cup, and plate; he had to learn his book; he had to go to church . . . ."

Main Idea (question 3)

Details (question 4)

Details (question 4)

Comprehension Assessment (cont.)

4. Choose **two** supporting details from those below to add to the graphic organizer on the previous page.

   A. People respect what Tom and Huck have to say.

   B. Huck's money earns interest.

   C. Huck feels shut in all the time.

   D. Huck feels like he is bound hand and foot by civilization.

5. Which statement best expresses one of the themes of the book?

   E. Children should be seen and not heard.

   F. Exploring caves can be fun.

   G. Growing up requires making important decisions.

   H. Society is always exactly what it seems on first glance.

6. What detail from the book provides the best evidence for your answer to number 5?

   A. Tom decides to testify at Injun Joe's trial.

   B. Judge Thatcher admires Tom.

   C. Widow Douglas wants to take care of Huck.

   D. The students plan a clever prank on the schoolmaster.

7. What is the purpose of this sentence from the book when Tom and Becky are in the cave: "But hunger and wretchedness rise superior to fears in the long run."

   _____

   _____

   _____

   _____

8. Which other quotation from the story serves a similar purpose?

   E. "Tom kissed her, with a choking sensation in his throat."

   F. Becky "had sunk into a dreary apathy and would not be roused."

   G. Tom "felt willing to risk Injun Joe and all other terrors."

   H. Becky "told Tom to go with the kite line and explore if he chose . . . ."

Name _____

Date _____

Response to Literature: Tom's Life—Your Life

Overview: Below are facts about life in a Missouri village during the late 19th century.

- Most people in the United States lived in villages or on farms.
- People grew or raised much of their own food.
- Most people made their own clothing. Most children had only one school outfit, one play outfit, and one church outfit. They were often barefoot.
- Children attended school in one-room schoolhouses. Many children had to quit school to work before completing sixth grade.
- Children in cities often worked in factories. Children as young as 9 or 10 worked in coal mines.
- Racism was common.

Directions: Think about these questions: How have things changed since the late 1800s? How have they stayed the same? Which way of life (then or now) do you think is better and why? What is your responsibility for making change? What is the government's responsibility for making life better? What are your hopes for the future?

Write an essay that follows these guidelines:

- State your opinion on the current state of life in the United States. Specify if you are writing about small towns, cities, or life in general.
- Write at least 750 words.
- Include main points, such as the changes over time, the responsibilities of government and individuals, and your hopes for the future.
- Draw upon what life was like in *The Adventures of Tom Sawyer* and current events.
- Provide a conclusion that summarizes your point of view.

Name _____

Date _____

Response to Literature Rubric

Directions: Use this rubric to evaluate student responses.

	Exceptional Writing	Quality Writing	Developing Writing
Focus and Organization	☐ States a clear opinion and elaborates well. Engages the reader from the opening hook through the middle to the conclusion. Demonstrates clear understanding of the intended audience and purpose of the piece.	☐ Provides a clear and consistent opinion. Maintains a clear perspective and supports it through elaborating details. Makes the opinion clear in the opening hook and summarizes well in the conclusion.	☐ Provides an inconsistent point of view. Does not support the topic adequately or misses pertinent information. Provides lack of clarity in the beginning, middle, and conclusion.
Text Evidence	☐ Provides comprehensive and accurate support. Includes relevant and worthwhile text references.	☐ Provides limited support. Provides few supporting text references.	☐ Provides very limited support for the text. Provides no supporting text references.
Written Expression	☐ Uses descriptive and precise language with clarity and intention. Maintains a consistent voice and uses an appropriate tone that supports meaning. Uses multiple sentence types and transitions well between ideas.	☐ Uses a broad vocabulary. Maintains a consistent voice and supports a tone and feelings through language. Varies sentence length and word choices.	☐ Uses a limited and unvaried vocabulary. Provides an inconsistent or weak voice and tone. Provides little to no variation in sentence type and length.
Language Conventions	☐ Capitalizes, punctuates, and spells accurately. Demonstrates complete thoughts within sentences, with accurate subject-verb agreement. Uses paragraphs appropriately and with clear purpose.	☐ Capitalizes, punctuates, and spells accurately. Demonstrates complete thoughts within sentences and appropriate grammar. Paragraphs are properly divided and supported.	☐ Incorrectly capitalizes, punctuates, and spells. Uses fragmented or run-on sentences. Utilizes poor grammar overall. Paragraphs are poorly divided and developed.

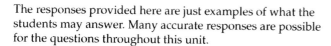

The responses provided here are just examples of what the students may answer. Many accurate responses are possible for the questions throughout this unit.

During Reading-Vocabulary Activity—Section 1: Chapters 1–8 (page 16)

1. Tom is **melancholy** because he wants to play, and there is a lot of fence to whitewash.

2. Sid always seems to be protected from getting punished. Opinions may vary regarding how fair this is.

Close Reading the Literature—Section 1: Chapters 1–8 (page 21)

1. Answers may include the murmur of the students; the air is "utterly dead"; there is nothing stirring; and it was "the sleepiest of days."

2. Cardiff Hill has soft green sides tinted with purple and a few birds and sleeping cows.

3. The tick has no reason to be happy as Tom begins to turn it around with a pin rather than letting it be.

4. Answers could include the tick being moved around due to the pin, the quiet room causing Tom to use the tick to amuse himself, and Joe deciding to join the fun with the tick because of his boredom.

During-Reading Vocabulary Activity—Section 2: Chapters 9–17 (page 26)

1. The boys had made predictions of how people would respond, and the boys were happy to see people shedding tears, being remorseful, and talking/reminiscing about the boys.

2. The tale is **pathetic** because it is a touching story about each boy, and the stories make people sad that the boys have drowned.

Close Reading the Literature—Section 2: Chapters 9–17 (page 31)

1. Tom sees a cool grey dawn, a quiet forest with dew on the leaves and grasses. The fire is going slightly, with a bit of smoke rising.

2. Tom believes that he will get new clothes because a worm climbed onto his leg. He also believes that ladybugs instinctively know about fires.

3. There are several birds mentioned in the passage—a catbird, the northern mocker, and a jay—indicating that it would be a good place to bird watch.

4. The "fox" squirrel "had probably never seen a human being before and scarcely knew whether to be afraid or not."

Close Reading the Literature— Section 3: Chapters 18–22 (page 41)

1. The biggest boys and the ladies aged 18 and 20 escape the lashing. They probably escape them because they have either learned how to please the schoolmaster or because they, particularly the boys, are too big physically.

2. The schoolmaster is bald and wears a wig. He is middle aged.

3. The schoolmaster boards with the boy's family, and the boy has many reasons to hate him.

4. The schoolmaster's wife will be gone, the master will be "fuddled," and he will nap in his chair.

Making Connections—Section 3:
Chapters 18–22 (page 42)

1. Answers will vary. Dilemmas may include telling the truth about sneaking home, taking the punishment for Becky, and pranking the schoolmaster.

During-Reading Vocabulary Activity—
Section 4: Chapters 23–28 (page 46)

1. To "give a **wide berth**" means to keep a good distance from something. The boys skirt the area of the haunted house, afraid of getting too close, especially because it's at night.

2. The house is silent, lonely, falling apart, ragged, and covered with cobwebs.

Close Reading the Literature—Section 4:
Chapters 23–28 (page 51)

1. Tom feels as though the dreams "happened in another world, or in a time long gone by."

2. Tom has "never seen as much as fifty dollars in one mass before."

3. He thinks of dimes or dollars as treasure. He's saved marbles, a doorknob, string, and other small items in the past.

4. Tom needs to find Huck to figure out if his adventure is only a dream or if it is a reality.

Close Reading the Literature—Section 5:
Chapters 29–35 (page 61)

1. Most of the people in the village live simply and are not rich.

2. The boys are admired and stared at. They are considered to be remarkable. The paper has written about them and includes biographical sketches of them.

3. The two boys' income is described as "simply prodigious" and is more than what the minister receives each week.

4. Tom saves Becky's life, lies for her, and takes the whipping for her at school. The judge says that "no commonplace boy would ever have got his daughter out of the cave."

Comprehension Assessment (pages 67–68)

1. C. spiteful

2. H. Becky "resolved to let him get whipped
. . . and to hate him forever."

3. Main idea: Huck's new life makes him miserable.

4. Supporting Details: C. Huck feels shut in all the time. D. Huck feels like he is bound hand and foot by civilization.

5. G. Growing up requires making important decisions.

6. A. Tom decides to testify at Injun Joe's trial.

7. When you are miserable and hungry, you get over your fears and are willing to take risks.

8. G. Tom "felt willing to risk Injun Joe and all other terrors."